Sweet Dreams

LESLIE SHERIDAN

SWEET DREAMS

This book is written to provide information and motivation to readers. Its purpose is not to render any type of psychological, legal, or professional advice of any kind. The content is the sole opinion and expression of the author, and not necessarily that of the publisher.

Copyright © 2019 by Leslie Sheridan

All rights reserved. No part of this book may be reproduced, transmitted, or distributed in any form by any means, including, but not limited to, recording, photocopying, or taking screenshots of parts of the book, without prior written permission from the author or the publisher. Brief quotations for noncommercial purposes, such as book reviews, permitted by Fair Use of the U.S. Copyright Law, are allowed without written permissions, as long as such quotations do not cause damage to the book's commercial value. For permissions, write to the publisher, whose address is stated below.

Printed in the United States of America.

ISBN   978-1-949746-99-0   (Paperback)
ISBN   978-1-64552-000-9   (Digital)

Lettra Press books may be ordered through booksellers or by contacting:

Lettra Press LLC
18229 E 52nd Ave.
Denver City, CO 80249
1 303 586 1431 | info@lettrapress.com
www.lettrapress.com

"Goodbyes are only for those who love with their eyes. Because for those who love with heart and soul, there is no such thing as separation." ~ Rumi

Contents

First Inklings 1
Janie 3
Grandma Shirley 11
The Afghan 21
Starting Over 27
Frankie 35
The Visitation 47
Signs – 1996 49

First Inklings

I was fourteen years old when I awoke in the middle of the night with the radio on. Whenever I had difficulty sleeping, I would leave the radio on for company. That night I was listening to WBCN, a rock radio station in Boston. Growing up I loved listening to rock music. It just made me feel good and transported me to another realm away from the pressures of high school and the general anxiety teenagers felt. That night I was having trouble sleeping and the radio provided the background music to the thoughts that kept me from falling back to sleep. As I lay in my bed tossing and turning I looked out of my bedroom window on that starry night and wondered: What happens to us when we die?

My parents were both raised catholic (my mother was Italian and my dad Irish), but brought my brother, Brian and me up Episcopalian. We were both baptized in the Episcopal Church, took communion and read from the Book of Common Prayer each Sunday and attended Sunday school. It was in church that I learned we all have souls inside of us and when we die our souls leave our bodies. How they did that I didn't know but they did. I understood that they went up to heaven, in the sky, but I was confused. I was thinking of the logistics of every human being who ever lived and died from the ancient Egyptians – who to my teenage knowledge were the earliest humans on earth – to that night and the poor souls who would die in the future. How would all those souls fit in the sky? Wouldn't it get crowded? I imagined souls packed side by side and one on top of another like books on a library shelf that went on forever.

And I gleaned from those church sermons that if we didn't get saved, we would go to hell. I expressed this concern to my parents, so then my brother Brian would taunt me on the Sundays when I didn't want to go to church. He would say, "If you don't go to Church today, Rosie, you're gonna go to hell." I envisioned a frightening place at the core of the earth with red hot flames and deep, dark inescapable caves. Then my logical side spoke up. Really? I thought, could there actually be a place worse than living on earth with war, poverty, people abusing others and themselves, murders, animals being tortured, starvation and hatred.

That year Jimmy Carter was president; the beginning of an epic classic, Star Wars flew into theatres; the punk rock group, The Sex Pistols released their debut album; Atari introduced a new video computer; and both Groucho Marx and Elvis Presley died. I didn't know it then, but it was also the year I had that first inkling about what happens to our souls that would ignite a spark and eventually start me on a spiritual odyssey.

Janie

*J*anie and I are going to the Round and Round record store to buy 45's and albums and I'm in a hurry because I am late picking her up. There is no answer when I knock on her front door so I open the door and call out to her as I run towards her bedroom in the back of the house. She is not there. I ask if anyone is here. No one answers me. No one is at home. Where is everyone? I notice that my heart is beating faster as I hurriedly look in the other rooms to find her. We have to get going to the record store. I run down the hallway away from her bedroom toward the front door and that is when I see her. She is lying on the floor behind the front door, blood staining the white carpet. Oh my God! She was not there when I came in less than five minutes ago. Was she?

Gasp! I wake up. My heart is beating so fast, practically through my chest. When I get my bearings I realize I am in my bed and I have just had a nightmare. Just a nightmare.

Rrrrinnngg. Fourth period has just ended. European History is not my thing. I walk to my locker, dial the combination, open it up, plop my books on top of all the others on the bottom, grab my lunch from the top, slam the locker door closed and walk down toward the cafeteria. Between the heads of other students heading to their next period class, I see Janie at her locker. She is putting away her books, grabbing her paper bag lunch and her sixth period books. She has Biology on the other side of the school. Lunch is only one of four classes that we have together scattered throughout the day. We pass notes to each other in the hall between the other periods. The notes have song lyrics that are going through our heads during class; boys; what new or older records we want to buy; anything that is bothering us – school or personal. Depending on how boring the class is, we will write only a sentence or three pages. On most days one of us will write a full page. It's sometimes surprising to me that we had so much to say to one another but it was fate that brought us together.

Janie sees me walking toward her. After shutting her locker, we walk together to the cafeteria. "Rockin' Rosie Mahoney, look at this!" she exclaims as she hands me the latest copy of Hit Parade magazine. The magazine is chock full of pictures of cute rock stars, some posing gorgeously with their big hair. "I'm really starting to get into this new band", Janie tells me, as she points to their picture on the front cover. "Def Leppard", she says.

Sweet Dreams

"I don't think I've heard of them", I say. I was still rebelliously in my punk rock phase.

"You should check them out, they sound great!" she says. Rock music was one of the common links between Janie and me. Janie and I have been friends since ninth grade. We met at lunch recess. During lunch periods when most of the students were done with lunch or if they did not eat lunch they would hang out in the hall near the cafeteria and the school store where they could buy chips, candy or cookies to eat as lunch. The cafeteria and the school store were near the front entrance to the school which had a large lobby with very high ceilings and the doors at the top of the stairs leading into school were generally left open during that time. The sound of students talking, laughing and yelling reverberated off the lobby walls and it was so loud; like a huge swarm of bees. I could barely hear my thoughts. It was there in that humming hallway that I first noticed Janie. She was holding her books and there was a drawing of a lightning bolt, a reference to Ace Frehley, the guitarist for the rock band KISS on the book cover of the bottom book. So, I walked up to her.

"Are you a KISS fan?" I inquired. "Yeah. You?" she replied. And just like that our friendship was born. But it would stay a friendship as long as Ace Frehley was not my favorite band member, she told me - sort of jokingly. Paul Stanley, the lead singer and guitarist had already been declared my favorite so I thought we were good.

Janie preferred to be called that name because it has more of a rock and roll sound than her given name. She is known in her Italian-Irish family as Jeanine. She looks like a rock star too: dark brown, feathered on the sides that framed her round face and fell just past her shoulders. Her staple rock ensemble consisted of a rock band *du jour* t-shirt, black leather jacket, black jeans and black ankle boots or Keds. She loved rock and roll and aspired to be a drummer. She had a drum lesson every week and practiced every day after school in her basement. In school she played air drums. She would do a long drum roll and announce my entrance at the lunch table. "Ladies and Gentleman: Rockin' Rosie Mahoney!" *Cymbals crash.* I looked more like the punk rocker: jeans, ripped in the knees, a striped shirt or occasional rock t-shirt and Converse All-Star high top sneakers. My hair was shorter than Janie's, pixie-style and just as dark as hers. Janie would say my blue-green eyes were like a mood ring: if my eyes were blue I was in a good mood, and if I was in a bad, evil mood they would flash green. Today they were blue.

I nicknamed her "Spacey" after "Space Ace" Frehley as he was called. Spacey and I would hang out and talk at lunch about everything: our dreams, records we bought or wanted to buy, personal things, school and boys – pretty much what we wrote about in the notes we passed. I sat down with both legs under the table and Spacey straddled the bench facing me while she went on about her drum lessons, rock bands and the cute guy she saw in one of her classes that day. I start to tell her about someone I had met at a track meet the previous Friday.

Oh God! Why did I mention that? She smiled her Cheshire cat smile and her brown eyes started to twinkle. "What's his name?" she asked. "Eric", I said just looking at her. Her eyebrows went up, waiting for his last name. "Eric. What's his last name?"

"I don't know." I told her. I explained he was the brother of someone on my track team. We hit it off, talking about...what else...music. He asked me if I had been looking at his muscular arms. Yes, he said that. His arms didn't impress me. It was actually his Led Zeppelin concert t-shirt that did. We carried on a conversation about concerts and how different college is from high school and he asked me what colleges I was applying to. I told him I wanted to stay in Massachusetts. It was kind of exciting talking with a slightly older boy. I felt more grown up. Janie said I should write him a letter.

"He's at U CONN. I don't have his address." I complained with the hope of being able to talk my way out of writing to him. I should have known better. Janie was an expert at following up when it came to boys. "Come on, Rosie!" He's a college man and you're a mature high school junior. It'll work. I've done it. I'll tell you what to write and then you mail it to him in care of the university." she instructed. "Okay." I said weakly. I was not confident flirting with or talking to boys unless I knew what I was talking about; basically I was awkward around boys. With any luck he would not receive it and I would be off the hook. So, I wrote the letter and mailed it, not expecting a reply from him. I couldn't believe it. He was glad I wrote and said he hoped to see me at the next track meet, maybe sooner. I called Janie and told her. "See!" she said. "I told you."

Janie was my best friend. She could make me laugh without trying and I was happier being with her than with anyone. We knew we could tell each other anything and both of us knew our secrets were safe with the other. Our friendship was effortless and natural.

One Saturday after we got back from the Round and Round record store in the mall, we were hanging out in her bedroom listening to a couple of the new records and 45's. Janie was suddenly and uncharacteristically quiet. It was unusual for her, but I just thought she was reading the liner notes of one of the new records. She became very thoughtful and had a concerned look on her face.

"What's wrong?" I asked her. "Rosie, I just had a premonition that I'm going to die." She said it very quietly, it was almost eerie. She didn't explain the premonition but I could tell that she was quietly questioning herself if it was real or imagined. I knew she wasn't kidding. "What are you talking about?" I said nervously playing with my sneaker laces, suddenly remembering the nightmare I had of her dying. I did not tell her about my dream. I never asked her what she saw in her premonition and she didn't offer. We didn't talk about it again.

There were endings and beginnings the next year – our senior year. I was deciding which college to go to. Janie was still taking drum lessons. She was still not sure what she was going to do after high school. John Lennon had been murdered that December. I think it was the first shocking loss of someone all of our peers knew. Ironically, the single from his next album was titled "Starting Over."

After graduation in June, I said goodbye to my teachers and classmates promising to keep in touch and left to start the next chapter of my life full of hope and believing I would have a successful future as a Physical Therapist. Janie and I stayed in touch over the summer. I was working as a waitress at the diner and getting ready to go to Boston University in August. Janie was hooking up with a local rock band, playing drums and singing. I had heard her play drums in her basement. She had it – I knew she would be great. I told her to tell me when and where they would be playing so I could see the band. The band, as yet unnamed, was still in their garage phase.

Janie practiced with her band most of the summer and my mom and I shopped for things I would need for my dorm. Janie and I would go out to see a couple of concerts together in a club in Boston; we were both 18, the legal drinking age. A few weeks later in mid August I called her house to see if she wanted to hang out before I left for college. That was a phone call I will have impressed upon my memory for as long as I live.

A male relative of Janie's who picked up the phone told me that she had been killed in an automobile accident the night before. I think my heart stopped. Now my heart was beating fast and I could not breathe. I felt as if I had just been kicked in the stomach. I felt numb. I tried to catch my breath.

When I could finally talk, I asked him, "What does that mean?" I knew what it meant, but the words echoed inside my head. I was in shock. Not Janie. No. No. No. He gave me the calling hours at the funeral home and hung up.

School friends, followed by friends of the family, and Janie's band mates arrived at the wake. I honestly don't even remember walking into the funeral home. I was numb from sadness and disbelief. It was so surreal. I do recall standing in the entryway, though, cautiously looking around into each side of the funeral home once I was in there. I was looking for Janie. Alive would be preferable and I would know that I was just dreaming this incredibly painful moment of my life. I walked around slowly. I saw friends of ours and Janie's mom but I couldn't talk. Talking would make it real and I didn't want this to be real.

Stefanie, a classmate of ours, came up to me, "I knew how close you and Janie were and I just wanted to be here for you. It's unreal, isn't it?" We hugged each other and tears fell from my eyes and down my cheeks and onto her curly, dark brown hair. Through my tears, I sighed and thought to myself, *it's real*.

Finally, I found Janie in an open casket. *Oh my God!* Her mom had put some of her favorite rock memorabilia and her drum sticks in the casket with her. She looked peaceful. Her head of beautiful dark brown hair was lying on a pink satin pillow. I looked at her face for a long time hoping she would wake up. Then I touched her hands that were holding her rosary beads. They were cold and I whispered to her, "I'll warm you up, Spacey."

It wasn't just sadness and grief that I was feeling. I was still in shock. Up to that time I had not lost anyone close to me. Death seemed so final. It was the end of her life and the end of our friendship. The End.

The next morning, my mom and dad and I went to her funeral and then to her mom's house afterwards. When I walked into her house there were so many people, mostly family. I gave her mom a hug. I felt sad for her: first her husband was gone and now her only child. Then, I walked uneasily toward her bedroom. It was as if I was walking through a tunnel slowly. I'd walked from Janie's front door to her bedroom so many times, but this time was much different. It was surreal walking into her room. I had a flashback of my nightmare. This was where we had hung out and listened to the latest albums. Her turntable and albums were on a shelf near her bed. I noticed two records that she had bought recently: Journey's "Escape" and Billy Squier's "Don't Say No". The plastic covering was still on them. Everyone knew music was what bonded us as friends. Her band mates, her cousins and Stefanie were in her bedroom. Someone put on a KISS record. It was so strange to be in her room listening to her records without her there.

I could say it was a rock band that brought Janie and me together. It may seem strange that that was the main thing we had in common to begin with. But, maybe a spark is all it takes to ignite a true friendship. There were so many questions going through my mind. Why did Janie have to die? What did it mean? Why were we friends for only a short time? I've heard that everything happens for a reason. I wish someone would tell me why. I knew I would never have another best friend again. My world just ended.

Grandma Shirley

After Janie died that summer, I became very depressed. She was my best friend. I didn't know how I was going to go on or what I was going to do now. I would never see her or talk to her ever again. Going to college would be a constant reminder that we weren't going to be together on the weekends or Holidays. I didn't want to stay in Massachusetts. I packed up a suitcase, left a note for my parents and brother saying goodbye and that I was taking a train to Phoenix to visit Grandma Shirley. Since I was deferring college, for now, I took my graduation money to pay for the train ticket. It was time for a change, a new perspective.

The 1980's were a decade of big change: Ronald Reagan was elected president for two terms; big hair and headbands; bustiers and spandex; people who wanted their MTV; the Sony Walkman; video games; and "E.T. The Extra Terrestrial" had everybody phoning home. On the train I thought Janie was right: Def Leppard were going to be big. Their new single "Bringin' on the Heartbreak" was getting a lot of airplay. Punk rock seemed to be waning in popularity, making way for new wave and the new wave of heavy metal.

Several hours later, as the train rolled out of Chicago where I changed trains, I thought of the changes I was seeing across the country from city to city and town to town. I thought how far away I was from home and all that had happened in the last few weeks. I knew that this was the best thing for me right now – rolling on to a new scene. The flashing scenery and hum of the train was relaxing and put me to sleep.

I woke up the next day as the train was crossing the border into Arizona heading south toward Tucson. I collected my things and my thoughts, put on my headphones to my Walkman and listened to Billy Squier's "Don't Say No" music cassette. It was the first time I had listened to it since Janie died. The tears started to flow and I didn't stop them. As I listened to the music I closed my eyes, put my head back against the seat and thought of Janie. I thought of the way she rolled her eyes when something was ridiculous, and the way she demanded I press the push button to the water fountain because she was holding too many books and couldn't do both. Once I held down the push button for her and assumed the position of a Greek goddess statue. She rolled her eyes at me.

The train pulled into the station in Tucson less than a week since leaving eastern Massachusetts. It felt longer than that and further away. The air here was hot and dry. I spotted Grandma Shirley. "Come here little one." She threw her arms around me and gave me a great big bear hug.

We got in her car and jumped on I-10 heading northwest to Phoenix. She asked me how the train ride was, if I enjoyed the scenery and how the food was. I told her everything was good, but I was starving. Grandma smiled and nodded her head as she drove.

Grandma Shirley's house was white stucco house with red shutters; not much of a yard, not like back east. We had grass in Massachusetts. Here in the desert it is mostly a mixture of sand and dirt, some cactus and mountains in the distance. It got very chilly at night in contrast to the scorching heat during the day. Inside her home was warm and welcoming. She had basic furniture but it was what she did with it that really made her home so interesting and relaxing at the same time. Grandma travelled a lot with her husband before he died. They travelled all across America, Canada and Europe. She had a few antiques in her home, as well as rugs, tables, vases and photographs: mementos of their life together. After my dad went to college and married my mom, Grandma and Grandpa Mahoney did some travelling and found that they loved Arizona. So, they bought a house and made a life there. Since my grandfather's death fifteen years ago, Grandma Shirley does not travel a lot. She knits, volunteers her time to various charities and bakes for their events and has become a fabulous cook, an interest she developed from her world travelling. It is some of that cooking that I smell now and my stomach starts growling.

"Roseanne", she calls me by my given name, "would you like to unpack your suitcase and get your room set up?" I follow her to my room, put my suitcase on the bed and unzip it. She shows me the dresser and closet. The bed has already been made for me. I thank her.

"When you are unpacked come out to the kitchen. I'm making Ratatouille."

One late afternoon Grandma Shirley and I were in her kitchen baking cookies. She said that she understood my being upset about my friend's loss. It had been about six months since Janie died. Her passing was still fresh. But, honestly, I was tired of being depressed and was starting to get bored with myself. She told me not to forget her but it was time to move on and paused a moment before she continued. "Our loved ones are not really gone when they pass away."

I shot her a "What are you talking about?" look. Janie was dead, I was at her funeral. She's gone. Grandma Shirley never raised her voice; she was always calm and self-assured. "Have you ever heard about re-incarnation, Roseanne?"

"No." I replied as every hair on my body stood up. I just looked at her.

"We all have souls inside of us. When our bodies die, our souls leave our bodies. It happens to everyone who dies including grandpa and your friend." She looked at me and I looked back at her lovely round face with beautiful blue eyes and light brown hair. I love and respect my grandma. She is a worldly woman and very intelligent. But, I didn't know what to say. I was confused. She stated this so confidently that I thought it was the truth and I should know this. I did not learn about re-incarnation in church. Was this her truth or *the* truth, I wondered. She sensed my confusion and explained.

"Have you ever experienced déjà vu? You could be at school, at home, in the supermarket or anywhere and maybe a feeling will come over you that you've been here before or already done this." I said that I had and she continued. "That's your soul remembering a past life you had in that place or with that person. You may not have seen that person before in this life, but one day you'll have a déjà vu moment. You've had a connection with that person in another lifetime. Or it could be your soul remembering that you planned this moment to meet that person before being re-incarnated in to this life."

While she was talking, I sampled a few of her cookies. When I finished chewing I said, "Janie had a vision when I was with her one day that she was going to die. I didn't ask her what the vision showed her. It kind of scared me."

Grandma explained, "She may have had a déjà vu moment where she saw what her soul already planned prior to coming into this lifetime."

There was one more thing I wanted to tell her. "Grandma, I had a dream that Janie died." I told her about the dream I had where I went to Janie's house and could not find her and then when I did find her lying on the floor in a pool of blood. "But, Janie actually died in a car accident. Is my dream the reason she's dead? You know, did I make this happen to her in my dream?"

Grandma Shirley explained. "That was a prophetic dream, dear. Your dream itself did not make her accident happen. Your subconscious was showing you a traumatic event while you were sleeping: a premonition of your friend's death. She died in a car accident, but there was blood around her when she died and it was sudden just like in your dream. The vision she had was a precognitive experience or a premonition of her death while she was awake; her subconscious knew it already. Speaking of dreams, I must be off to bed."

Grandma told me she had a doctor appointment in the morning and would be bringing her cookies to the Elk Lodge for a luncheon and not to eat them all. "Sweet Dreams, Roseanne."

Grandma had given me food for thought. I took a small plate of cookies and a glass of milk to my bedroom.

In bed that night I tossed and turned. I turned on my radio like I usually did when I couldn't sleep. Grandma Shirley gave me so much information that I couldn't process. First, she was religious. Second, I didn't know she believed in this new age spirituality. Obviously, something changed since I had last seen her. Perhaps she learned about it while travelling or as a way to understand grandpa's death.

Whatever, I had heard of déjà vu. But, I thought it was just a colloquial phrase. This soul remembering thing was new to me. What exactly is a soul? Does it have a brain? I'm a left brain, logical human and I just could not wrap my mind around this concept. Or, was it simply that it defied the religion that I was brought up on and perhaps I was using it to block out this new age spirituality as my grandma called it. Reincarnation, déjà vu, souls and prophetic dreams were new ideas to me. This was the stuff of science fiction but strangely it didn't frighten me that much. I was intrigued but it was a lot to take in.

I'm sitting with a woman a little older than me. Her hair is blonde, falling just to her shoulders. We are sitting across from each other in a small cubicle and she is arranging a deck of cards, but they're not ordinary cards. They have cups and swords and strange names like Pentacles. She is talking to me but I can't really hear her. I understand her, though. She is telling me about the cards and what they represent in my life: love life, money and career. Then she reveals the death card. It's upside down. She tells me that my grandmother is anemic and that she needs to listen to her doctor and do everything her doctor tells her to do and she'll be fine.

After my grandma got home that afternoon she told me we were having steak and roasted vegetables for dinner tonight. No fancy meal for dinner that night she said. I helped her clean and cut the green beans, red pepper and sweet potatoes. She told me that her doctor told her that she is a little anemic and she should increase her iron. *Déjà vu.* Hmmm. That sounded familiar. I had noticed that she had been feeling a little tired lately. She wasn't her usual active self.

After dinner, I told her I would clean up the dinner dishes and she could go relax. She went into the living room, turned on the television and sat in her recliner. Her girls – 'The Golden Girls' – were on that night. She picked up her knitting needles and her emerald green yarn and continued knitting an afghan that she had been working on. I thought about how lonely she must be living alone without grandpa. She tried to keep herself busy with her volunteer work and game nights at the Elk Lodge. It must have been hard some days to come home to an empty house.

When I was done cleaning up in the kitchen, I made both of us a cup of tea and joined her in the living room. We watched television and talked for a little while longer and then she said she was heading off to bed with her 'sleeping pill'. Her sleeping pill was a book – whatever one she happened to be reading at any given time – on her nightstand. For her it was like a drug. She would read a few paragraphs, maybe a page and then fall asleep.

The next day, Grandma went to the hospital to read to the patients where she volunteered twice a week. While she was out, I called my dad at work. There is a three hour time difference between Massachusetts and Arizona. He asked me how I was doing and what I was doing and how was the weather and when I would come home and begin going to college. Rather than answer all of those questions, I asked him how everyone back home was doing. We talked for a few more minutes and then I mentioned that Grandma Shirley didn't seem herself. She seemed tired and a little slow, which for her meant she wasn't baking as much and sat in her recliner, knitting, more often. He was quiet and thoughtful for a moment and then he said he hoped to see me come home soon. I said okay, give mom my love and hung up.

When grandma came home from her volunteer job, I told her that I would probably be going back home soon. I told her about the phone call with my dad. She seemed a little sad because she had become so used to me being there, but she understood it was time for me to move forward. I wasn't sure I was ready to go back home. I felt I was being pushed to get on with my life.

"Roseanne, let's eat out tonight. Would you like to go shopping first?" she asked. We went shopping at the mall. I was a little nervous about going home. I would just be reminded of Janie and everything. I explained this as we were walking around the mall. She looked at me and said, "You know, Roseanne, you're stronger than you think. You can go on. So, let's get you some new clothes for your new beginning, shall we?" She didn't have to say it twice. What woman doesn't love clothes shopping?

When we got home that night, I hugged and thanked my grandma for dinner and the clothes. I brought my clothes to my bedroom, looked them over, and hung them up in the closet. I went out to the living room and said good night to her. She was watching television and knitting orange yarn into her afghan. "Sweet dreams, Rosanne", she said to me with a smile.

I'm in a dance aerobics class. I'm teaching the class and I know the people there. There is a lot of energy in the class. I feel that I'm not home in Massachusetts, though. I feel that I'm in New York City! In my dream I know that it's time to go home.

Sweet Dreams

I wake up. I *know* it's time to leave Arizona and go back east, to start a new life in New York City.

It's 6:30 in the morning. My grandma is already awake, having her tea and reading the newspaper outside on the patio. She looks so relaxed. As I look around the spacious patio and look up at the cloudless blue sky, I understand why she likes it here. I've seen her meditate out here some mornings, except today. I tell her about my dream and that I'll be leaving in about a week. She says that she would like to come with me. We would take an airplane together and she'll take care of the plane reservations. She called my mom and dad and let them know we'll be flying out the next week.

It was a rainy Saturday afternoon when we touched down at Logan Airport. My mom, dad and brother, Brian, were there to greet us. We drove an hour west of Boston with the rain barely letting up. How different from the arid environment of Arizona. I went downstairs to the kitchen to help my mom with dinner. She was making my favorite meal: ziti parmagiana with homemade meatballs. I really missed her cooking. And, then at the dinner table with my family around me I dropped a bombshell.

"I've decided that I want to go to New York. I could stay with Aunt Julie and Uncle Vito in Brooklyn and work in their restaurant while I find other work there. I don't want to stay in Massachusetts anymore."

I gave them my decision and proposal. I took a deep breath and waited for the storm to hit. I could see it on both of my parents' faces. They stopped eating and looked at me and then each other. Everything got real quiet for less than a minute but it seemed longer than that.

Finally, my dad spoke. "Why do you want to go to New York City?"

"I don't think my future is here. I want to go to New York."

Then my mom calmly asked, "Rosanne, what will you do there other than work in Aunt Julie's restaurant? When will you go to college?"

I don't know if I understood their concern. I was more interested in taking charge of my own life. They were both college educated and I know how important a college education was to them. It could guarantee me a successful, stable life.

"Rosie," my dad said patiently looking in my grandma's direction, "we understood that you needed time and you went to visit grandma in Arizona. Isn't a year enough time? It's time for you to stop wandering and get serious."

"I need to try New York. I want you to believe in me. I want you to trust me."

My mom asked me where the idea to live in New York came from. I couldn't explain to my parents that I had a dream that showed I was in New York. If I said I had a dream, they would interpret it as desire. How would I tell them that I had a precognitive dream? I knew I could talk freely about spirituality with Grandma Shirley but I still didn't grasp new age spirituality so how would I explain it to my parents. But, if I did understand it enough to articulate it to them, they wouldn't listen. They were both brought up in the church. This new age spirituality would freak them out or anger them or both. It wasn't exactly in the mainstream and I wasn't ready to go out on that limb yet.

The Afghan

My bags were packed and I was excited to begin a new life in New York City. My family was disappointed that I would not be attending college...again. They understood that it was my life and I needed to try this. I think Grandma Shirley said something to them on my behalf because they were talking for quite a while in the den. When my dad came out he had a concerned look on his face and my mom was visibly upset. They told me that I should go to New York and give it a try; but that I could come home any time I wanted. Dad told me to go upstairs and say goodbye to Grandma Shirley.

I found her in her bedroom. She was packing her clothes into her suitcase. "May I help you pack, Grandma?"

She looked up at me and smiled. "I'm nearly packed, thank you, dear." After a moment she said to me, "I have something for you, Rosanne. I finished it last night." She handed me the afghan she started knitting when I began my near year long visit with her in Arizona. She had knitted every color of the rainbow into the afghan blanket finished off with a white border.

"Every color of the rainbow - it's beautiful!" I could not believe she knitted this just for me.

"Yes. These colors are also the same colors of the Chakras – the body's energy centers." she added.

She described where they are on the body and that I can meditate on them whenever I need to and maybe that would be something I might want to learn about sometime.

"Each color corresponds to a part of the body. For example, the green chakra" she said as she touched the green color that I had seen her knitting, "is at your sternum and is the color of love, happiness, and prosperity."

I opened the blanket to hold it up and see all the colors together: red, orange, yellow, green, blue, indigo and violet. Roy G Biv. That's how I learned the colors of the rainbow in science class in school. The border of the blanket was white: all the colors together make white. I knew that a prism refracts light. Light goes through one side of the prism and spectrum colors, rainbow colors come out the other side.

"Thank you, grandma. I will cherish this forever." I said as I hugged her. She gave me her big bear hug and held it a little longer. I started to fold up the blanket and picked up the envelope that fell out of it. On it was written: "When the student is ready, the teacher will appear."

"That is an ancient Buddhist proverb. When you have time, you can read it. I believe you are embarking on a spiritual journey."

I was about to embark on a journey to a new life in New York, I still wasn't sure about all this new age stuff. I loved my grandma very much. I loved being around her and in her home.

Sweet Dreams

It's so peaceful and restorative to be near her. But, it wasn't just the new age ambivalence I was feeling. Moving forward felt right. Something else did not feel right. I couldn't quite place it.

Grandma's flight was at six o'clock the next morning. Dad brought her to the airport before he went to work. That night at dinner mom and dad told me that grandma had been diagnosed with leukemia. She was going home to take care of some things and move back here. My dad would fly out next week and help her pack things up and fly back with her.

On the bus ride to Brooklyn, I opened the envelope in my backpack that read, "When the student is ready, the teacher will appear." I took out several pages of folded paper. I unfolded the paper and counted five pages of lined writing paper with my grandma's penmanship. I put my headphones on, tuned WBCN on my Walkman and read the letter. At first the rock music playing in my ears was background music and as I kept reading I heard only my grandma's voice talking to me; the music was drowned out.

> My dear Rosanne,
>
> I told you a little bit about re-incarnation when you visited me in Arizona. I understand it may feel strange to you. However, I want to share this with you. This may help you understand your prophetic dreams more.
>
> We've had lives before with people who are currently in our lives. We don't necessarily have consecutive lives with them – although sometimes we may. It depends on what we need to learn from each other and the experience. Each individual has different experiences

within one lifetime with different people. For example, I chose to have a specific lesson – let's say perseverance. My soul or higher self chose this before my incarnation into this life. Each soul plans their life as a human on earth with their spirit guides, angels and the loved one or loved ones that will help on the journey.

Let's compare it to a meeting with your guidance counselor in school. You talk about your plans for college: what course of study you want to learn, what classes you'll take, which college you want to go to. Then there are the people involved in the planning: you, your guidance counselor, your parents, your friends perhaps, and the administration at the colleges you apply and get accepted to.

Now…let's go back to my story. My parents, siblings, my husband (grandpa), my children (your dad and Uncle John), my grandchildren (you and Brian), and my friends were all chosen to assist me at various stages of my journey before I incarnated into this life. So, my soul and spirit guides and angels create a "blueprint" of how my mission on earth is going to go. I know I made that last sentence sound like I'm an alien. I think you've known me long enough to know that I am not!

So, everyone knows the plan: my spirit guides, angels, me (my soul or higher self), and one or more of the above, depending on which phase of my life I am living. This is true for everyone. Can you recall how busy your guidance counselor was when he or she was preparing you and your classmates for college?

There is always a "clause" in the "blueprint". It's called free will. This is where the soul can make a choice to defer a lesson. God has given us this gift. We can always stick to the plan, or we can choose to do it later. If we choose to do that lesson later we can defer it to another time, but, the chance to learn that lesson will come up again. My advice: don't defer it to another life, you're here now – do it and have it over with.

Our soul's choice to incarnate into a human body is an opportunity for your soul to do accelerated learning. Our souls "learn" lessons where they are on the other side (or heaven as most people know it) but they don't learn at the rate that souls in human form do. The courses here on earth are harder, trickier and we learn the lessons faster here as a result, generally, unless we defer or fail and have to do the lesson again.

Your souls choice to defer college and visit me in Arizona and again to move to New York, I believe, is because you may have chosen to let life teach you through experiences in different places and with different people rather than learn lessons in a classroom. Only your higher self and spirit guides and angels know for sure. Whatever path you choose, it's always a good idea to educate yourself: read, experience things and travel.

Rosanne dear, I am confident that you will find more "teachers" on your spiritual journey as you go through your life. I wish you a life filled with happiness and love and joy!

Love and kisses,
Grandma

Starting Over

Something feels right about moving to a big city. I really liked the idea of losing myself in a concrete jungle. I wanted to completely block out any thoughts of new age spirituality, Janie and Grandma Shirley for the time being. It was all too much. A few hours after leaving Massachusetts, again, the bus pulled into the depot. My Aunt Julie met me there and we go back to her house. It's a large brick house with spacious rooms. I get myself mostly unpacked and Aunt Julie and I go to her restaurant, Mangia! Aunt Julie is mom's older sister. She and her husband, Uncle Vito, opened their restaurant about thirteen years ago. I remember my mom, dad and Brian and me coming to eat here when it opened.

Aunt Julie introduces me to the other girls who wait tables and then has me start working by clearing tables and restocking the condiments. This is just what I wanted: to be so busy that I can't think. The next day I start waiting tables. It is hard work and my feet are killing me by the end of the night, but the tips are good. I am grateful to my aunt and uncle for giving me this job and I express gratitude by working as hard as I can. I want to show them that I've earned this job through hard work and dedication, not just because I was their niece.

I took my three o'clock pre-dinner break and it would be the only thing I would eat until after the evening rush. Aunt Julie said it would be busy tonight because it was an unseasonably mild fall day and they generally had a lot of customers on days like this. I was sitting down at a table near the kitchen eating a plate of penne pasta with parmesan cheese when another of the evening waitresses, Pamela, came in to start her shift. She was about my height, 5'10", straight brown hair and green eyes. She was wearing the standard white shirt and black slacks and the non-standard layers of jewelry. I liked that she wasn't afraid to express herself.

"Hi. I'm Pamela", she said.

"Roseanne. You can call me Rosie. It's nice to meet you."

"You're Julie's niece. We'll be working together tonight."

Pamela took me under her wing. She introduced me to the other evening wait staff, bus persons, and cooks. Whenever we were working the same shift, Pamela and I would have a few minutes to talk and we got to know each other pretty well, and after our shifts we would sit at the bar and talk and laugh a lot. We like the same music, movies and worked out at the same gym. I had joined a gym shortly after arriving here and wanted to work on becoming a certified aerobics instructor. Partly because of the dream I had and partly because I was athletic in high school and was going to study to be a Physical Therapist in college. I just wanted to see which way this path would take me.

Sweet Dreams

Pamela worked out at the gym a few days a week. She worked out to keep up her stamina for waitressing and for her dance career. She had danced in smaller parts in shows on Broadway and had been in a show in London's West End recently for about six months. She went on auditions and was waitressing until she got her big break. Her dream was to be a principal dancer in a big Broadway production. We were together so much that a few customers in the restaurant asked us if we were sisters. We did look alike: we both had dark hair and we were the same height.

After a couple of months things were going well for me in the Big Apple. I was making good money in tips and I finally became a Certified Aerobics instructor. I taught a class five days a week and continued to work at the restaurant every day. And I still had time to go out with Pamela a few nights a week. When we went to see the Ramones at CBGB's, Pamela got a drink at the bar and the bartender asked what her sister wanted. We both laughed and told him we weren't sisters.

The Christmas and New Year's holidays were coming and I told Aunt Julie that I would be going home for a week or two. I had talked to my mom and dad every week. Grandma Shirley had moved in with them after I moved to Brooklyn. Her and my dad had flown to Arizona and sold her house and some of her possessions and packed up what didn't sell and shipped them back to Massachusetts. Grandma had leukemia. My dad told me this would be her last Christmas with us.

On the bus ride home, I turned on my Walkman, listening to the music as I tried to recall all the times I had been with my grandma and all the fun my brother and I had with her and how lovely she was and how I loved cooking and baking with her and the words of wisdom she imparted to me. Her and my grandpa brought back souvenirs for Brian and me. We were mesmerized by the stories of their travels. We felt as if we'd been in all of those places with them. She taught me that cooking in the kitchen would increase my confidence. She always said the more you do something the better you'll be at it. And it was true for everything in life, not just cooking. I reflected on my time in Arizona with her and our conversations about spirituality. I was trying to understand it. I wasn't sure if it was because I was more aware or if it was meant to be, but suddenly things were opening up for me in many ways. It was as if where I started there was a blue line and I just kept following wherever it led me. True, there were sad moments and fabulous opportunities. When one door closed, another one opened.

Grandma Shirley started her spiritual journey after my grandpa died. She meditated and practiced yoga in her spare time. It's almost as if she had been preparing for this very moment in her life. I saw the end of a person's life as final. She said it wasn't. Our souls go on. I really wanted to believe that they did. I was glad I still had Grandma Shirley to talk to because I had so many questions to ask her. I would ask her where our souls go when it leaves the body. How will I know our loved ones are near us after they die? Would I see them – like a ghost? How long will they be around for?

I hoped she wouldn't die before I had a chance to talk to her.

Of all the conversations Pamela and I had, I never brought up re-incarnation. Something kept me from asking her how she felt about it or if she'd ever heard of it. Religion and spirituality seemed like taboo subjects to bring up unless you knew the person you were talking to was a devout Christian or if you were in church. Our spiritual and political beliefs were personal or so I had been taught. I think the thought of asking Pamela if she believed in reincarnation and seeing her look at me like I was a freak, would crush me. I didn't want to risk our friendship over it.

We all went to church on Christmas Eve. Grandma Shirley sat between me and my dad. We helped her to stand up if she could. It must be hard for my dad, I thought, to see his mom so sick and knowing this would be the last Christmas with her. I remembered what she told me at the mall in Arizona before we came back east. You can go on.

Christmas day was wonderful. Everyone wanted it to be that way for grandma. We opened presents, ate all day and spent the later part of the day watching "It's a Wonderful Life" on television. When the movie ended I helped grandma to her room, tucked her in bed and read her a couple of pages from her 'sleeping pill' until she fell asleep. I kissed her on the forehead. "Sweet dreams, grandma", I said, closed the door and went to my room.

I took the blanket she knitted for me and wrapped it around me and imagined it was a big bear hug from grandma. I laid down in a fetal position on my bed and the tears fell down across my nose and down the side of my face. My pillow felt wet. Janie was gone. Grandma would be gone, too. At least I could prepare myself for her death. I cried myself to sleep.

My mother, sister and I are sitting in a covered wagon. It is cold and this journey is long and the path is unstable. As I look out the front of the wagon, my father is in the seat behind the horses. Ahead of the horses I see many other covered wagons. We are part of a convoy but I'm not

sure where we are going. My sister is older than me and she is protecting me on this journey. There's a strong feeling about her.

Now we are in California. I feel that this was our destination. But I am here only with my sister. My parents are both dead; they did not survive the journey west. My sister and I are in San Francisco. We are domestics. We make our living by cleaning houses. I am so upset about the loss of our parents, especially our mother. I cannot get over her loss, but my sister does and she is able to move forward.

I wake up from my dream. It felt real. I find paper and a pen to write this down so I can ask my grandma about it. I write down some of the details so I won't forget them. The dream is not in color, but a brownish color, like a very old photograph that has faded. And my sister was Pamela.

Later that day I told grandma about my dream. She looked at me with surprise in her eyes. She smiled and said, "Ah, this is proof for you that re-incarnation is real. This is a past life recall dream. So the details in your dream are real or were real. The California gold rush of the 1800's perhaps? And the girl in your dream was your sister then. Who is she in this life?"

"Pamela – she's a friend in New York. That's so weird. People have asked us if we are sisters. We're both tall and have dark hair but that's where our similarities end."

"You were meant to meet again in this life time. There's a reason for everything, Rosanne. From now on you should keep a dream journal. You have a lot of interesting dreams, dear. Not all dreams are past life or prophetic. Some are a way of getting our attention. They can point us in the right direction or help us to understand things that are happening in our waking lives. It may help you to get a dream book, too" she suggested.

Grandma Shirley died peacefully in her sleep the day after New Years.

I am grateful for the time I spent with her. The night I told her about my past life dream with Pamela, she told me she was ready to go. She was looking forward to seeing her husband again and her mother and father. She lived a full life with no regrets and she wasn't scared. Grandma told me it was natural to feel scared and be sad.

"I will miss you" I said, tears streaming down my face.

"I'll be around. I'll pop in from time to time for a visit", she said smiling weakly.

"Wherever your soul goes, tell me what it's like when you visit me."

Frankie

*J*went back to Aunt Julie's and back to work. I felt a little empty, but kept busy. It was the mid – 1980's: I had been out of high school for a few years, decided not to go to college to the dismay of my family; and was now living with my aunt and uncle in Brooklyn and working at their restaurant nearly every day. I resumed teaching aerobic and step aerobics classes at the gym. I was starting to feel like it was time for something new. Not a change, just something to make me feel fresh and alive.

Pamela introduced me to the owner of the dance studio and her dance instructor, Frankie. "So you want to learn to dance?" he said, looking straight at me. He was aloof and very serious. If I were a professional dancer with a career in the balance I would have been intimidated.

"I'm an aerobics instructor and I want to take some dance lessons to enhance my classes; to change things up a little." I explained.

"Okay, let's see what you can do."

Pamela was stretching and gave me a wink, letting me know everything was good, while Frankie went to put the music on. When he came back, he and Pamela started dancing and I did my best to keep up. We danced for about five minutes, when he stopped. He asked me when I wanted to start lessons. I told him Monday. Pamela smiled and nodded her head in the affirmative. I sat in a chair at the back of the room while she finished her lesson.

As we left to go back home, she said, "He really likes you. I think he was impressed with you."

"Really, I couldn't tell. He seemed a little standoffish."

"Well, he likes you or he wouldn't have asked you when you wanted to start lessons." I thanked Pamela. She just smiled at me.

It was exciting to start something new. The dance lessons knocked me out of my same old routine of just working at the restaurant and teaching aerobics classes. Aerobics kept me fit. I knew I could dance and I could incorporate more dance routines in my classes to make them more fun and varied rather than doing repetitions of various movements. So, I went into Manhattan a few days a week to take Jazz and Modern dance classes. This turned out to be the most interesting turning point in my life.

Frankie teaches several dance classes for adults and students of dance: Ballroom, Waltz, Jazz, Modern, Tap. Some of his students have become successful on Broadway. He was a dancer and choreographer on Broadway for many years but quit professional dancing when he found his talents were better spent teaching others the art. He clearly loves dancing; he is very passionate about dancing and is totally focused and disciplined. He expected me to work hard whether or not I was aspiring to have a dance career.

We always begin class by stretching, stretching, stretching. I have found that dancers have long legs because they stretch their hamstrings a lot, but this practice keeps them flexible and agile. I love the dance classes. It was great to be taking a class and enjoying it; teaching a class is rewarding, but not that relaxing. When I teach, I'm instructing, thinking about what is next in the class, watching the participants – are they doing the steps safely and correctly?

I think he saw potential in me and after a few classes suggested that I try out as a background dancer for a musical he was choreographing. I laughed because I thought he was joking. He looked at me with a straight face. We were just becoming friends and I hadn't yet realized that he didn't joke about anything.

"I want you to come here tomorrow morning and try out. I believe you can do this" he said it as if it were a command. Did he know something I didn't? Well, I showed up the next morning and auditioned and I got one of the spots. Opening night was a little scary, but exhilarating at the same time.

I can't describe how I got here. Less than three years ago I was graduating high school and today I was a background dancer in a Broadway show. This was easy, unexpected and it felt right! Is this what I was I meant to be doing all along? I wished I could take a look at my "blueprint" now to find out.

The following week when I went back to the studio to practice my routine with Frankie, I expressed this to him. After our lesson, he said "Let's go down to the café and get some espresso." He said it as if he were a parent instructing his child.

Once we were in the café, Frankie ordered us espressos and biscotti.

Frankie told me he owns this entire building. He took his Broadway money and invested it in real estate. He opened the dance studio first and then found a couple who had run a café in his native Brooklyn, and asked them to manage Le Café Gratus.

Frankie is very simply an attractive man. He has short, dark wavy hair, a beard and mustache which are nicely groomed and close to his face. His watery blue eyes set against his dark hair and beard is stunning. His muscular dancer's physique and medium height had made him desirable to Broadway producers….oh and yes, his talent, too. He reminded me of Gene Kelly, but with darker hair and a beard and minus the smile. Frankie mainly smiled with his eyes, when he smiled at all. He was serious, his mind was always working and he preternaturally knows things.

"You're a talented dancer, Rosanne. I'd like to see you do music videos" he said. Was he acting as my agent, too, I wondered? "You'll have to get an agent. I know someone, I'll get you the phone number", he added.

"Did you just read my mind" I asked him incredulously.

"Not exactly but I get things about people."

"What do you mean?"

"I wouldn't feel comfortable talking about this with anyone else, but you did mention how dancing "just" happened for you. You didn't work hard to get here – dancing, that is – but you got here. That's what I would call destiny. You were meant to do this, now, with me, at this time."

Every single hair on my body stood up. I think my short hair was standing up by itself without the help of any hair product. "You sound just like my grandma Shirley. Are you going to tell me that this is all part of something we planned before we each re-incarnated?"

Sweet Dreams

He was smiling with his eyes again and I think I saw his lips curl up just a little. "Yes."

"So, you believe in re-incarnation and the soul goes on after this life?"

"Yes, I do. You don't entirely believe it, but your grandmother did?"

I nodded yes and told him what my grandma told me. I briefly explained Janie's death and the dream I had before she died and other prophetic dreams I've had; the conversations I've had with my grandma; the afghan she knitted for me and how I knew I had to be in New York and how everything progressed from there.

Frankie very patiently listened to me, then nodded his head and said, "I have a class coming in a half hour. We can talk more about it tomorrow – are you free in the morning?" I nodded that I was. "Come to my apartment at 10:00, we can talk more then. Get a good night sleep." He gave me a kiss on the cheek and we left the café.

Janie called me on the phone. "Rockin' Rosie Mahoney!"
"Janie! Where are you?" I cried.
"I'm in a safe, happy place."
"How are you?"
"I'm fine." She said she was calling me from a pay telephone and had to go.
Thank God, she's all right, I thought.

I woke up feeling more relaxed than I had in recent memory. It was like this sadness I've been carrying around was lifted off of me and no longer weighed me down. It was the first time I had dreamt of Janie since she passed away nearly three years ago.

I got out of bed and got dressed, brushed my teeth and washed up. I hailed a cab and was on my way to Frankie's Manhattan apartment.

I ring the bell to his apartment at the front door of his building. "Rosanne?" he inquires. "Yes." I reply. He buzzes me in and I run up the three flights of stairs – I like running up stairs because it feels like I am working out even when I am not working out. Frankie is waiting for me outside his apartment door. He gives me a kiss and hug hello and invites me in.

Frankie's apartment is tastefully decorated and has a warm, welcoming atmosphere and I feel like I never want to leave. I sit down on his white soft leather loveseat with plush blue throw pillows and I feel as if I've just been hugged, it's incredibly comfortable. The white and gold colored drapery is closed to keep out the invading sunshine from his balcony sliding glass door. The soft glow of a clear glass table lamp is the only light in his living room. I hear water running and notice his cherub water fountain in the corner opposite the sliding glass door. There was a serenity here that belied the busyness of a metropolis outside the front door. Now I get why Frankie is always so calm and peaceful. Living here would be restorative to me also.

Frankie handed me a cup of herbal tea. "So." he said with his smiling eyes.

"So, why did you ask me here?" I asked.

"I want to talk with you about what you've been experiencing lately. I feel a responsibility toward you." He said quietly and waited for my response.

"Me? Why?" I asked curiously.

"Because I believe I'm meant to. Everything happens for a reason, Rosanne. Everything we do, everywhere we go, and everyone we meet is for a reason. We are all put here for a purpose. And, I *feel* that I am meant to help you." He said very calmly.

I can't tell if he's hitting on me or if he's serious. I'm thinking I could cut and run, but I'm not getting a bad feeling about this. "What exactly do you want to help me with?"

"I want to help you spiritually. Not religiously, but spiritually. If you will allow me to." he said.

"Okay." I said as I shrugged my shoulder.

Frankie said, "There is an ancient Buddhist proverb that says 'When the student is ready, the teacher will appear.' "

Every hair on my entire body stood up when he said that - again. Grandma Shirley said the same thing to me. I thought back to our conversation in the café last night, while Frankie waited patiently for my response. I paused a moment and then suddenly realized I dreamt of Janie again last night. I told Frankie about the dream. "That can't be prophetic, though, because she can't physically call me anymore. So is that a wishful thinking dream?" I asked.

"No, it's not a wishful thinking dream. That was a visitation dream, meaning she did connect with you through your dream. The telephone is a means of communication. It takes a while to get a message from our loved ones who have passed on, sometimes." he said.

"How do you know so much about all this?" I asked him.

He told me, "I started my spiritual journey almost fifteen years ago. I was 17. I got a lot of resistance from my family about my career path and my sexuality. I wanted to find myself. I finished high school, went to college and things seemed to flow from there. When things flow and it feels right, it is right. Like, I found where I belonged and found my purpose. Dancing is how I learned to express myself. And it's who I am. I am a dancer, an artist and I'm content. I could have conformed to everyone's rules and probably ended up taking a destructive path. But, I chose to go a different way – my way. You and I have that in common. I went to yoga retreats around the country, I learned to meditate, and I travelled around Europe for a while. I discovered myself because this is the path my soul chose for this life time. That's it in a nutshell."

We both sat in his living room deep in thought with just the sound of the water flowing in the water fountain. I kind of understood him. I believe we all struggle with something. I liked Frankie as a friend. He trusted me with his story and I had a whole new respect for him because I know it could not have been easy for him. Frankie is quiet, calm, patient and graceful. Maybe finding himself helped him find peace. It's not easy to figure out what we're supposed to do with our lives when we're younger. It would be great if we could physically take our soul's blueprint with us on our journey. Would that be cheating? It takes strength and courage to go up against the crowd of those who want us to do what they want us to do. And if we are all on our own path, what right does anyone have to pass judgment on another?

I asked him, "Are you religious at all? Do you believe in God and creation and Jesus and heaven and hell?"

He looked at me directly and said, "I believe in a God force, I believe Jesus was on his own spiritual journey and it was his life's purpose to teach others about God. I believe there is a beautiful place we all go to when we leave our bodies and hell, well, we're living in it. Think about it: prejudice, hatred, war, famine, poverty, greed, fear. It can't get anymore hellish than that. I was raised catholic, but I don't believe in organized religion anymore."

I nodded my head as if to say, *I see*. I didn't really, but maybe that was a conversation for another day. We had talked about a lot over the last two days. I felt like I was in an advanced spirituality class. Anyway it was interesting to see this whole different side of Frankie. The more I listened to him, the more I understood. I think everything my grandma told me was starting to sink in or was this just my souls re-awakening?

Sensing that he may have started to overwhelm me, Frankie changed the subject and quietly said, "Tell me about Grandma Shirley and Janie."

I took another sip of my tea and put the tea cup on the coffee table. I sighed and sat as far back as I could into his loveseat and made myself very comfortable before I spoke. "Janie's death was real hard because it was the first time I lost someone close to me and because it was unexpected. Music was really the only thing we had in common, but I was happy being around her. She was wicked funny, she didn't like school and had she lived I think she would've been a rock star. She knew what she wanted to be. Grandma Shirley was older, obviously, and sick, but I miss her terribly. She was wonderful. She taught me life skills like balancing a check book." I took a sip of my tea while Frankie looked at me patiently and waited for me to continue. "You know Janie had a vision one day that she was going to die, but I never asked her what the vision was. I think I was too scared to know what it was. I wish I had asked her. And I had a dream about her dying almost a year before she passed away." I described the dream to Frankie. "Janie died about a couple of years ago and my grandma died just after New Year's this year."

He nodded. "I'm sorry for your losses. But knowing that our soul's go on should lessen the pain a little. They're not here with us physically, but they are around us. Believe that."

"I really wish I could believe that, Frankie. But, it just doesn't seem logical to me. How do I get to the point where you are? How do you know for sure our loved ones are around us? I mean, maybe that dream I had last night was a coincidence. And, how can you swear off Christian religion so easily and just believe in this new age spirituality?"

Frankie actually smiled with his lips! Was I imagining this?

"Rosanne, my dear friend, you just said the magic words."

What magic words? I thought.

"Just believe" he said as if he'd read my mind. "You just believe. Spirituality is about feeling rather than relying on the intellect. Anytime you catch yourself analyzing anything, just stop yourself and go with your feelings rather than using logic. Try it sometime."

About an hour later I told him I had to go. He understood. But before I left he walked over to his bookshelf and took out two books and handed them to me. "Homework: read these." He handed me Shirley Maclaine's "Out on a Limb" and Edgar Cayce's "There is a River." "Everyone starts somewhere on their spiritual journey. Namaste." We hugged and said good bye.

I walked down the stairs and out the front door and hailed a cab. I gave the cab driver the address I wanted to be driven to and put the headphones to my Walkman on. There were thoughts swirling through my mind as the taxi drove me through Manhattan and back to Brooklyn. What was my purpose? What is the meaning of life? Why can't we see our deceased loved ones if they're around us? Frankie gave me a lot to think about.

Upstairs in my bedroom at Aunt Julie's house, I browsed through the books Frankie gave me. I started to read "Out on a Limb" until I fell asleep.

The next day I couldn't stop thinking about him and what he'd said. I thought I might drop by his studio to see him but it could wait until my lesson the next afternoon. I went to work in the restaurant that night. After work, upstairs in my bedroom, I read more of the books he gave me. They were very interesting but a lot to take in.

"Out on a Limb" which had just come out, was the story of Shirley Maclaine's starting point on her spiritual journey. She started out as a dancer as well. That was interesting to me. The book "There is a River" was the story of Edgar Cayce, also known as the Sleeping Prophet, had precognitive dreams and visions while he was in a trance. He had all of his dreams and visions written down, most of which were for clients who wanted answers to their questions regarding their health. I put the books down and tried to go to sleep. I wanted to talk to Frankie some more about spirituality; I was happy and relieved to have someone to talk to about it.

After teaching my morning aerobics class, I went over to the studio a little early. It was my night off from the restaurant, so the rest of the day was mine to do what I wanted. When I walked into the studio, Frankie told me there was a music video that we would be in. He had already arranged it and today we would be working on the routine for it. We had become very good friends and now we were to be dance partners.

"We?" I asked.

"Yes, you and I. They were looking for a couple to do a ballroom dance routine." I didn't think I needed to check my souls' blueprint to know this was meant to be. I just felt it was.

The Visitation

J recall lying on the left side of my body on the side of my bed that is closest to the window. I was asleep. I can clearly see my sage green bedroom walls with rose wall paper trimming. I see my dresser on the right side of my window with my jewelry box, framed photographs and a small lamp.

There is someone sitting on my bed near my feet. The vision is ethereal, beautiful and pure white. I know that it is a woman. I see streams of white circling around her. It is part of her. She is talking to me but I cannot hear what she says, although I hear her telepathically. I can see her moving her head a little as she speaks. And then, I feel her touch my leg.

"I told you I would pop in from time to time, Roseanne. I have been around you. I see what you have been doing and you are doing well for yourself. You asked me to tell you what it's like where I am. Well, it is

beautiful and peaceful. There's no such thing as pain or fear here, only love and joy.

It didn't hurt when my body died. The human body housed my soul for its journey on earth. My soul left and I went up towards the sky. The other side isn't really in the sky, only a different dimension. My soul went through a blue tunnel. The tunnel was lined with people I knew, angels and my spirit guides. I felt only love. Grandpa was waiting for me.

There's no such thing as time here but things do happen much faster here than on earth; kind of like time lapse photography. There is lightness here unlike the density of the third dimension of earth.

There are beautiful gardens and fountains here. There are beautiful temples here. In one of them I went for a past life review. My spirit guides accompany me while I review the life I just finished. I review everything I did or didn't do; opportunities that came to me that I did or did not take advantage of. Everything is for the soul's growth: did the soul accomplish the lessons it wanted to learn? There are also pets that have crossed over, too. By the way, Frankie is a nice man.

She kisses me on the cheek. Startled, I wake up and lift my head off pillow. Was it a dream? Or was it real? I am lying on the left side of my body on the side of the bed that faces the window. I look at the window. I look at my dresser with my framed photographs, jewelry box and a small lamp. And I see my sage green bedroom walls with a rose wall paper trim. Then I look at the end of my bed. "Grandma?"

Signs – 1996

When you try to find something, you won't find it. Conversely, when you aren't looking for something, it'll find you. You'll get a sign that a loved one is around you and think that it's nothing or it's just a coincidence. Then, the nudges start; that nagging feeling that we need to do or pay attention to something. Spirit or our loved ones don't give up easily. We'll keep getting nudges and signs that we need to be doing something and we'll keep getting them in various ways. Spirit doesn't give up because the message is important.

I had learned from Frankie to educate myself on all things spiritual. We meditated together and went on retreats together. I even tried practicing to be aware. He became my spiritual mentor. We still worked together in dance. I had a career turn that was unexpected. Frankie and I started a new business together involving all aspects of spiritually oriented programs. I wondered what would have happened if I hadn't paid attention to my dreams or had guidance from Grandma Shirley and Frankie. I journal my dreams as my grandma suggested. I would be living an entirely different life. I know the life I have now is the path I am meant to be on because everything about it feels right.

So one recent rainy spring day I was driving home to Massachusetts to visit family. I received one of the best gifts ever from a crossed over loved one on the Massachusetts Turnpike.

Driving about 50 miles an hour with a Billy Squier CD playing in my car I notice a utility truck directly in front of me. It wasn't speeding up or changing lanes and I slowed down a little to avoid an accident. I also didn't change lanes. I begin to realize that maybe I am meant to stay in this lane. Then I start to feel as if someone is telling me to look at the back of the truck. Okay, I think, I'm looking. What am I looking for? *"No, look. Really look."* I get a knowing rather than hearing a voice, but it's weird because I think I can almost hear a voice. Now, I feel that my head is being held in place to look straight ahead, like a horse with blinders on. Still not getting it, apparently, because now there's a soft focus around words I am meant to see. It read "SPACEY HEATING AND PLUMBING." Still nothing. I'm still cruising at 50 miles per hour and the next song on the CD plays: "In the Dark". And I did feel in the dark. Why would I need the name of a plumbing and heating truck and their phone number? Everything feels like it's in slow motion until I get what is going on. It's the word SPACEY standing out while the other words and phone number are completely blurred out. SPACEY…. SPACEY?? SPACEY!! Oh my God!! Spacey.

It's Janie!! I was crying and laughing at the same time. Janie chose this truck to deliver a message to me. She chose a truck with her high school nickname on it to get my attention. I believe she just wanted to check in and say hello. It took me about fifteen minutes to get that message. No doubt she rolled her eyes at me. This was another way I learned that our loved ones can reach out to us from the other side during our waking hours. Of course there are the coins and feathers, too. But Janie was having some fun. Nineteen year earlier I wanted to know what happens to our souls when we die. Now I know that our loved ones never leave us. Sometimes we just need to be aware of our senses and watch for signs.

Back in Manhattan, I talked Frankie into going with me to the final concert of KISS's reunion tour at Madison Square Garden. "Why am I coming with you to this concert?" Frankie asked me as we walked arm in arm past the marquee and up the steps toward the arena.

"Hmmm. Men in make-up, high heels and spandex. You wouldn't enjoy that?" I said jokingly.

"Actually, I had a dream that Janie told me to look for her playing air drums."

www.ingramcontent.com/pod-product-compliance
Lightning Source LLC
Chambersburg PA
CBHW050204130526
44591CB00034B/2130